BOOK WORMS

Transformations in Nature

A Tadpole Becomes a Frog

Amy Hayes

T0014545

Cavendish
Square

New York

Published in 2016 by Cavendish Square Publishing, LLC
243 5th Avenue, Suite 136, New York, NY 10016

Copyright © 2016 by Cavendish Square Publishing, LLC

First Edition

Website: cavendishsq.com

This publication represents the opinions and views of the author based on his or her personal experience, knowledge, and research. The information in this book serves as a general guide only. The author and publisher have used their best efforts in preparing this book and disclaim liability rising directly or indirectly from the use and application of this book.

CPSIA Compliance Information: Batch #CW16CSQ

All websites were available and accurate when this book was sent to press.

Cataloging-in-Publication Data

Hayes, Amy.
A tadpole becomes a frog / by Amy Hayes.
p. cm. — (Transformations in nature)
Includes index.
ISBN 978-1-5026-0820-8 (hardcover) ISBN 978-1-5026-0818-5 (paperback) ISBN 978-1-5026-0821-5 (e-book)
1. Frogs — Life cycles — Juvenile literature. 2. Tadpoles — Juvenile literature. I. Hayes, Amy. II. Title.
QL668.E2 H39 2016
597.8'.9139—d23

Editorial Director: David McNamara
Copy Editor: Rebecca Rohan
Art Director: Jeff Talbot
Designer: Stephanie Flecha
Senior Production Manager: Jennifer Ryder-Talbot
Production Editor: Renni Johnson
Photo Research: J8 Media

The photographs in this book are used by permission and through the courtesy of: Savo Ilic/Shutterstock.com, Tom Reichner/Shutterstock.com, cover; Artur Synenko/Shutterstock.com, 5; Brian Mckay Photographyy/Moment/Getty Images, 7; E R DEGGINGER/Science Source/Getty Images, 9; Wil Meinderts/ Buiten-beeld/Minden Pictures/Getty Images, 11; Johner Images/Getty Images, 13; Ron Brancato/E+/Getty Images, 15; George Grall/National Geographic/Getty Images, 17; George Grall/National Geographic/Getty Images, 19; Photo-tistic/Flickr Flash/Getty Image, 20.

Printed in the United States of America

Contents

Tadpoles turn into frogs!

First, a mother frog
lays many eggs.

These eggs will
turn into tadpoles.

9

The tadpoles **hatch** from the eggs.

11

The tadpoles **swim** through the water.

13

As a tadpole grows,
it forms legs.

When a tadpole has legs,
it becomes a **froglet**.

17

The legs get longer, and the tail gets very short.

19

The tadpole has become a frog!

21

New Words

froglet (FROG-let) A tadpole with legs, also considered a young frog.

hatch (HATCH) To break out of an egg.

swim (SWIM) To move through water.

tadpoles (TAD-pohlz) Small creatures that turn into frogs or toads.

Index

About the Author

Amy Hayes lives in the beautiful city of Buffalo, New York. She has written several books for children, including *Hornets, Medusa and Pegasus, From Wax to Crayons,* and *We Need Worms!*

About BOOKWORMS

Bookworms help independent readers gain reading confidence through high-frequency words, simple sentences, and strong picture/text support. Each book explores a concept that helps children relate what they read to the world they live in.